Huguette Kirby

Transfer motifs for children

358 patterns to embroider or paint

Search Press

First published in Great Britain 2004 by
Search Press Limited
Wellwood, North Farm Road, Tunbridge Wells, Kent TN2 3DR

Originally published in France by
LTA, a department of Meta-Éditions
Original title: *Motifs de Transferts pour Enfants*
© LTA, a department of Meta-Éditions
Dépôt légal: April 2003
Photography: Charlie Abad

English translation by Norman Porter
English translation © Search Press Limited 2004

ISBN 1 84448 018 6

The Publishers and author can accept no responsibility for any
consequences arising from the information, advice or instructions
given in this publication.

Suppliers
If you have difficulty in obtaining any of the materials and equipment
mentioned in this book, please visit the Search Press website for details
of suppliers: **www.searchpress.com**

Alternatively, you can write to the Publishers at the address above
for a current list of stockists, which includes firms that operate a
mail-order service.

Acknowledgements
The publishers would like to thank DMC for the embroidery threads;
Loisirs et Creations for the heart-shaped box shown on page 9, the
gift bag shown on page 10, the t-shirts shown on page 12 and the
frames shown on page 11; Panduro for the small case shown on
page 9; Pébéo for the paints.

Printed in Italy by Canale.

Contents

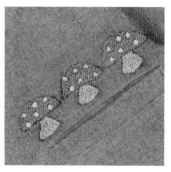

*D*ogs, cats, castles, dragons, dinosaurs, teddy bears, boats, sea creatures, elephants, hearts, flowers, fruit and alphabets. In these pages you will find a variety of easily created motifs which will delight children of all ages. The patterns, pictures and designs can be embroidered or painted on to clothes, soft furnishings or furniture. Discover how to make original gifts for family and friends: boxes, frames, notebooks, bags, jackets, t-shirts, dresses, jeans and much more. For best results, choose flat objects to ensure that the motif is properly transferred.

Huguette Kirby

How to start

The motifs in this book have been reversed so that they appear the right way round when transferred. They can be reproduced on fabrics, paper, card or wood, and are ironed on directly with a hot iron. This means you can easily decorate and personalise a child's bedroom with co-ordinating cushions, curtains and bed linen or adorn a wardrobe with dragons or dinosaurs. Then you can brighten up their clothes and toys with lively and amusing pictures, or embellish their bags and hats with delightful designs. The techniques are quick, simple and fun to do.

The motifs can be ironed on to most fabrics, but it is more difficult to transfer the designs on to finer fabrics such as silk. Always do a preliminary test. Motifs can be re-used five to eight times if you are using delicate material, or two or three times if you are using heavier material. The following instructions apply to working with fabric, and these can be adapted when working with paper, card and wood.

- First cut out your transfer design.
- Mark the position of the transfer on your surface using a soft pencil. On fabric, these marks will disappear when the fabric is washed. Any remaining marks on paper, card or wood can be wiped or rubbed away using an eraser.
- Small items can be placed on an ironing board. When using fabric, protect the surface with a piece of cotton to prevent the transfer marking the top of the board, then place the fabric on top of the cotton.
- Place the printed side of the transfer on your surface and secure, using pins for fabric and masking tape for other surfaces.
- Place paper over the transfer to protect it.
- You are now ready to iron the transfer. Never use a steam setting. Set the iron to 'Cotton' and press carefully. Gently raise one corner of the transfer to check that the motif has printed properly. If the image is not clear, repeat the process. If it has printed correctly, remove the transfer.

Practical tips

Repeating motifs

Simple motifs can be easily transformed into borders or corner designs. In order to visualise what a border will look like, place a mirror vertically on your chosen motif and the reflected image will show you the design.

To create a corner, place the mirror at right angles to the motif. Mark this angle with a soft pencil and repeat the motif on the other side of your positioning marks.

Embroidery

• Positioning a motif

If you need to centre a motif, or motifs, you will need to do this before framing your fabric. Fold the fabric in four and tack as shown on the diagram opposite, or measure your fabric and using a pencil, lightly draw perpendicular lines on to the surface.

• Framing

It is advisable to work on a frame and an embroidery hoop is ideal if you are using one or two motifs. First bind the inner frame using 2.5cm (1in) wide cotton strips, then place your fabric over it. Position the outer frame on top and press down firmly so that the fabric is stretched taut. Turn the screw of the outer frame to secure the fabric. If you want to embroider more than two motifs, use an adjustable frame and always follow the manufacturers' instructions.

Positioning a motif

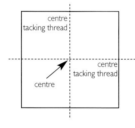

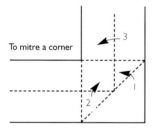

• Finishing off

To make hems for place mats, serviettes or other items, fold the edge of the fabric back 1cm (3/8in), then fold back again to make a 2cm (3/4in) hem. To mitre a corner, see the diagram above. Press all hems and corners.

• Caring for embroidery

Wash the embroidery by hand in soapy warm water. Rinse it gently without wringing, then allow it to dry flat. Always iron the embroidered material on the reverse side. To avoid crushing the stitches, place a damp cloth over the motif or motifs and press carefully with a hot iron.

• Method

The fabric is now stretched over the embroidery hoop and you are ready to stitch. When choosing your threads, you can use the colours suggested in the following pages, or select your own. Use a needle with an eye that will not leave a hole in the fabric. Choose the stitch or stitches you are going to use from the page opposite and start stitching. To start off, rather than make a knot in the thread, you can work the end of the thread into the design, beneath an area that has already been embroidered. When the work is finished, iron it on the reverse side, using a damp cloth.

• Finishing the work

Once the work is complete, stretch out the fabric on a piece of stiff cardboard or thin plywood and secure it with adhesive tape. You can soften the appearance by inserting a piece of flannel or felt.

Painting on fabric

You can paint on all types of fabric but you will need to wash and iron it first to remove the dressing. Choose white fabrics if you want to achieve a transparent watercolour effect and bright coloured fabrics for an opaque gouache effect. You can buy fabric paints in most arts and crafts shops. They are mostly thick and cover well so, to make them more transparent, use a thinning medium. Colours for relief painting are also available.

Place the washed and ironed fabric on a piece of protective paper which will also absorb any surplus colour. Now transfer the motif and

paint it. Allow the paint to dry for several hours. Press firmly on the reverse side with a hot iron in order to fix the colours.

Painting on wood

The surface to be painted must be clean and free from grease so, if necessary, rub it down with sandpaper. Use acrylic paints for painting on wood which can be found in most craft shops. These paints are matt and can be thinned with water or mixed with one another. They are easy to use and dry quickly.

Acrylic colours can be left as they are to give a vibrant look to the object but apply a coat of clear varnish to protect the surface once the paint is dry. Alternatively you can achieve a variety of finishes easily. To give the impression of age, or a patina effect, apply colourless wax to the dry painted surface. A gloss varnish will give a shiny finish. There are numerous products available which will help you create aged or crackled effects.

The projects in this book are intended as an inspiration and the techniques described can be applied to your own choice of furniture, toy boxes, wooden boxes, cardboard boxes, frames and more.

Embroidery stitches

BACK STITCH

Back stitch is embroidered from right to left with neat, small stitches, alternating between a forward stitch then a back stitch. Use for lines, outlines and curves.

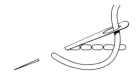

FRENCH KNOT

Bring the needle up through the fabric and loop the thread around the needle. Reinsert the needle just to the side of the knot. Gently pull the knot tight. More loops can be made for bigger knots. Use to embellish designs, as texture or as an outline.

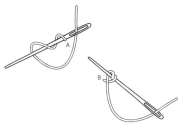

BLANKET STITCH

Blanket stitch is embroidered from left to right. Insert the needle vertically and pull the thread under it as shown. Pull the stitch tight gently. Repeat. The stitches should be regular and close together. Use for edging and decorative effects.

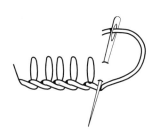

STEM STITCH

Stem stitch should be kept small and even. It is worked upwards as shown. Work one stitch then insert the needle into the fabric and take it out halfway along the first stitch. The thread must stay on the right of the needle. Use for curved and straight lines and for outlines.

SATIN STITCH

Satin stitch can be embroidered in any direction, but care is required to ensure that the outlines are accurate and edges neat. Bring the needle up and take the thread across the shape then insert the needle and take the thread back up. Work the stitches close together as shown. The fabric should not be visible between the stitches. This stitch is used to fill in small areas.

ENCROACHING SATIN STITCH

Encroaching satin stitch is not regular like ordinary satin stitch. The stitches where the thread enters and emerges are never on the same line. They can be worked as shown in the diagram below; alternatively, you can work long and short stitches together. You may want to change your thread colours to create a graduated effect. Use this stitch to fill in large areas.

CHAIN STITCH

When starting, bring the thread up then insert the needle at this point. Form a loop which must go underneath the tip of the needle. Bring the needle out again further along and repeat, making sure that the loop is the same size as the one before. Use this stitch for straight and curved outlines, edges and for filling in areas.

Painted projects

Heart box *Motif page 36*

MATERIALS

Heart-shaped cardboard box
Acrylic paints: white, purple, orange, yellow, turquoise
Large paint brush, small paint brush
Palette

METHOD

- Apply 2 coats of white paint to the inside and outside of the box allowing the first coat to dry for half an hour before applying the next.
- To paint the lid, mix half a teaspoon of purple paint with half a teaspoon of white paint.
- Apply 2 coats of pale purple to the lid.
- Apply 2 coats of purple to the box. Leave to dry for 1 hour.
- Transfer the motifs (see page 4), and using 2 coats of paint, apply the colours.

Dinosaur notebook *Motif page 44*

MATERIALS

Notebook with cardboard cover
Acrylic paints: white, ultramarine blue, light green, yellow, black
Large paint brush, small paint brush
Palette

METHOD

- Apply 2 coats of white paint to the outside of the notebook allowing the first coat to dry for half an hour before applying the next. Leave to dry for 1 hour.
- Transfer the motif (see page 4).
- Using 2 coats of paint, apply the colours, starting with the blue background. Leave to dry for 1 hour.
- Finish off with a black outline to define the motif.

Small case *Motif page 45*

MATERIALS

Small cardboard case
Acrylic paints: white, ultramarine blue, orange, pink, purple, yellow
Large paint brush, small paint brush
Palette

METHOD

- Apply 2 coats of white paint to the whole case.
- Mix one and a half teaspoons of yellow paint with half a teaspoon of white for the background colour. Apply 2 coats, allowing the first coat to dry for half an hour before applying the next. Leave to dry for 1 hour.
- Transfer the motif on to the lid (see page 4) and apply the colours.

Gift bag
Motif page 18

MATERIALS

Card bag
Acrylic paints: white, turquoise,
  ultramarine blue, yellow, black
Large paint brush, small paint brush
Palette

METHOD

- Apply 2 coats of white paint to the outside of the bag. Leave to dry for 1 hour.
- Transfer the motif (see page 4) and, using 2 coats, apply the colours.

Bears and hearts frame
Motifs pages 29-30

MATERIALS

Fabric frame
Fabric paints: white, purple, pink, orange,
  turquoise
Small paint brush
Palette

METHOD

- Transfer the motifs on to the frame (see page 4).
- Apply the colours and leave to dry for 1 hour.
- Cover the frame with a piece of cotton and press with a hot iron to fix the colours.

Snail frame
Motif page 34

MATERIALS

White wooden frame
Acrylic paints: white, yellow ochre, green,
  yellow, purple, orange
Large paint brush, small paint brush
Palette

METHOD

- Mix 2 tablespoons of white with a drop of yellow ochre and paint the frame with two coats, allowing the first coat to dry for half an hour before applying the next. Leave to dry for 1 hour.
- Transfer the motifs (see page 4) and paint them with 2 coats.
- Finish off with black outlines to define the motifs.

Flower t-shirt
Motif page 35

MATERIALS

White t-shirt
Fabric paint: white
Glossy fabric paints: pink, orange,
  green, gold
Small paint brush
Palette
White paper

METHOD

- Place the white paper inside the t-shirt where the motif is to be applied to protect the back of the garment.
- Transfer the motifs (see page 4) and paint them. Leave to dry for 1 hour.
- Remove the paper.
- Place a piece of paper over the pattern and press with a hot iron (not on the steam setting) to fix the colours.

Elephant t-shirt
Motif page 33

MATERIALS

White t-shirt
Fabric paint: black
Small paint brush
Sheet of A4 white paper

METHOD

- Place the white paper inside the t-shirt where the motif is to be applied, to protect the back of the garment.
- Transfer the motif (see page 4). Outline and paint in the details. Leave to dry for 1 hour.
- Remove the white paper.
- Place paper over the motif and press with a hot iron (not on the steam setting) to fix the colours.

Embroidered projects

The simple projects on this page are worked on linen and you should use stranded embroidery cotton. The rest of the projects are worked on clothes, also in stranded embroidery cotton. The colours shown here can be used as a guide, or choose your own. Wonderful effects can be achieved with metallic or variegated threads. The transfers will show up better on lighter coloured fabrics.

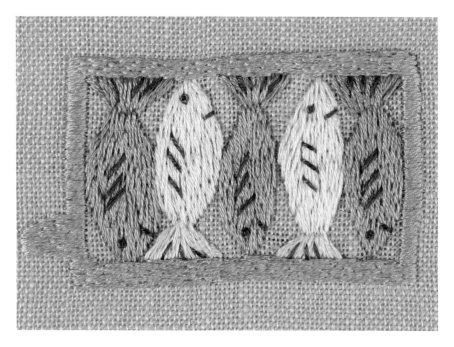

Fish
Motif page 40

Colours: pale yellow, yellow, green.
The border, the fish and the details on the bodies are embroidered with satin stitch (see page 7).
The eyes of the fish are embroidered with small French knots.

Flowers
Motif page 35

Colours: blue, yellow
The flowers are embroidered with satin stitch. The centres are French knots which have been worked with three loops.

Dungarees
Motif page 47

Colours: pink, blue, yellow, grey, red

- Stitches: back stitch, satin stitch. The lines are all worked in back stitch.

- Planet on the top pocket: outline in back stitch and fill in with satin stitch.

- Rocket on the right: use back stitch for the outline, the flames and stripes. Work the portholes in satin stitch.

- Rocket on the left: use back stitch for the outline and flames. Work the portholes in satin stitch, and the fuselage details in chain stitch.

Tortoise jacket
Motif page 34

Colours: light pink, dark pink, light green, green, dark green, ecru

Stitches: use satin stitch for all the motifs. Embroider each mouth with a small back stitch and the eyes with small French knots.

Mushroom jacket
Motif page 38

Colours: orange, green, ecru

Stitch: use satin stitch for all the motifs. Work each one individually making sure the edges are neat.

Dress

Motif page 35

Colours: green, purple, ecru, orange

Stitches: use satin stitch for the smaller flowers and encroaching satin stitch for the larger flowers. The centres are worked with small and large French knots, the latter using three or four loops, instead of one, depending on the size of the flowers.

31

33

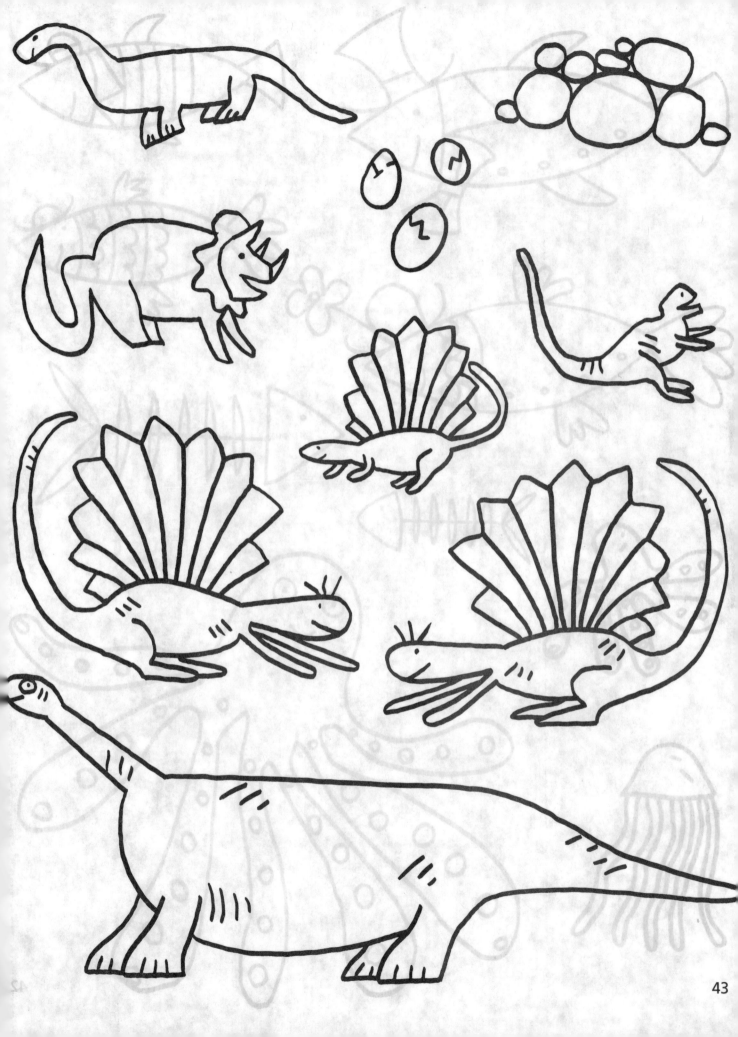

44

46